OCCASIONAL PA

TOWARDS A FIQH FOR MINORITIES

Some Basic Reflections

TAHA JABIR ALALWANI

NEW REVISED EDITION

TRANSLATED FROM THE ARABIC BY
ASHUR A. SHAMIS

THE INTERNATIONAL INSTITUTE OF ISLAMIC THOUGHT
LONDON · WASHINGTON

SECOND EDITION
FIRST EDITION, 1423AH/2003CE

THE INTERNATIONAL INSTITUTE OF ISLAMIC THOUGHT
LONDON OFFICE
P.O. BOX 126, RICHMOND, SURREY TW9 2UD, UK
WWW.IIITUK.COM

USA OFFICE
P.O. BOX 669, HERNDON, VA 20172, USA
WWW.IIIT.ORG

ISBN 978-1-56564-352-9

Typesetting by Sideek Ali
Cover design by Sohail Nakhooda
Printed in the United Kingdom by Cromwell Press Group

SERIES EDITORS
DR. ANAS S. AL SHAIKH-ALI
SHIRAZ KHAN

CONTENTS

FOREWORD

THE INTERNATIONAL INSTITUTE OF ISLAMIC THOUGHT (IIIT) London Office has great pleasure in presenting this revised edition of *Towards a Fiqh for Minorities: Some Basic Reflections* by Dr. Taha J. Alalwani. Originally published in 2003 as Occasional Paper 10, the paper calls for the development of a specific jurisprudence for Muslim minorities, particularly those residing in the West, taking into account the peculiar requirements of their condition and location. The study remains as valid today as when it first appeared.

"Fiqh for Minorities" is an important subject and a much needed contribution to an area of fiqh that has become essential for the well being and development of Muslim communities living in non-Muslim lands. Previous attempts to deal with the many serious issues facing these communities failed to take into consideration the views and contributions of Muslim social scientists who live in the West, speak its languages and have a comprehensive understanding of its social, political, religious and economic systems. As a result, many of the recommendations and fatwas that came to be issued were inadequate and in some cases complicated the issues under consideration. Dr. Alalwani's recommendation that existing fiqh councils should work closely with associations of Muslim social scientists and involve these scientists on an equal footing with Shariʿah scholars, not simply as cosmetic additions, is an essential step towards building a stronger and valid basis for the much needed perspective on fiqh.

The paper also calls for recourse to principles enshrined in the philosophy of *maqāṣid al-sharīʿah* (the higher intents and purposes of Islamic law). Indeed, knowledge of *al-maqāṣid* is a prerequisite for any attempt to address and resolve contemporary issues challenging Islamic thought. No doubt such knowledge can help in the process of developing a much needed objectives-based fiqh for minorities and is essential for anyone who is interested in understanding and appreciating the concept of divine wisdom underlying Islamic rulings.

Since few works in the English language have been available on the subject of *maqāṣid al-sharīᶜah*, the IIIT decided to fill the vacuum by initiating the translation and publication of a series of books and occasional papers on *al-maqāṣid* to introduce this important and difficult area of thought to English readers. These include to date, *Ibn Ashur Treatise on Maqāṣid al-Shariᶜah*, *Imam al-Shāṭibī's Theory of the Higher Objectives and Intents of Islamic Law* by Ahmad al-Raysuni, *Towards Realization of the Higher Intents of Islamic Law: Maqāṣid al-Shariᶜah a Functional Approach* by Gamal Eldin Attia, and *Maqasid al-Shariah as Philosophy of Islamic Law: A Systems Approach* by Jasser Auda. In addition, as the topic is a complex and intellectually challenging one, with most books appearing on the subject written mainly for specialists, scholars and intellectuals alone, the IIIT London Office has also produced simple introductory guides to the subject as part of its Occasional Papers series with a view to providing easy to read, accessible material for the general reader. These include *Maqāṣid al-Sharīᶜah Made Simple* by Muhammad Hashim Kamali, *Maqāṣid al-Sharīᶜah: A Beginner's Guide* by Jasser Auda, and *The Islamic Vision of Development in the Light of Maqāṣid al-Sharīᶜah* by Muhammad Umer Chapra.

In essence Dr. Alalwani's paper is really a call for Muslim minorities to have a sense of themselves as citizens and develop a positive, confident view of their place and value in society, moving away from notions of immigrant status. In broadening the concept of a fiqh for minorities therefore to a wider notion of a fiqh of citizenship we give recognition to the cultural and pluralistic milieu in which Muslim minorities find themselves, governed by a humanistic vision focusing on the betterment of society.

We hope that this paper with its innovative approach, analysis and ideas, will not only make an important contribution to the issue of developing a fiqh for minorites, but also attract wider attention and generate greater interest among readers.

The IIIT was established in 1981, and has served as a major center to facilitate serious scholarly efforts based on Islamic vision, values and principles. Its programs of research, seminars and conferences for the last twenty-eight years have resulted in the publication of more than two hundred and fifty titles under different series in English and Arabic, many of which have been translated into several other languages.

In 1989 the London Office initiated the Occasional Paper series, a set of easy to read booklets designed to present, in concise format, research papers, articles and lectures from the Institute's worldwide program as well as from scholars and social scientists willing to make contributions. To date fifteen papers have been published in the series the last of which was in 2008, with several being translated into French and German.

In conformity with the IIIT Style Sheet, *A Guide for Authors, Translators and Copy-Editors*, words and proper names of Arabic origin or those written in a script derived from Arabic have been transliterated throughout the work except when mentioned in the quoted text. In such cases they have been cited as such without application of the IIIT transliteration system. However, words and common nouns of Arabic origin that have entered into general usage are not italicized, nor written with initial capital.

We would like to express our thanks and gratitude to Dr. Taha Jabir Alalwani as well as the editorial and production team and those who were directly or indirectly involved in the completion of this paper: Dr. Munawar A. Anees (who revised this edition), Zaynab Alawiye (who revised the first edition), Sylvia Hunt, and Tahira Hadi, all of whom worked tirelessly in helping prepare the paper for publication. May God reward them and the author for all their efforts.

ANAS S. AL SHAIKH-ALI, CBE
Muharram 1431 AH, *January, 2010*

INTRODUCTION

MUSLIM theologians have produced a theology for the majority, but a systematic formulation on the status of being a minority remains to be developed. This essay by the distinguished Shariʿah scholar, Professor Taha Jabir Alalwani outlines a set of principles that he has considered essential for the proper exploration of the status of Muslims as a minority. He rightly points out that his use of the word "fiqh" in the title of this essay does not refer exclusively to what is called Islamic Law, but to what he, following Abū Ḥanīfah, calls "the greater fiqh." In other words, his project is aimed at providing a methodology for a broad development of Muslim thought in all areas bearing on theology, law, and even history. This is an ambitious but necessary under-taking.

The author, Chairman of the Fiqh Council of North America, is well aware that the challenges facing Muslims in the West are broader than the confined area of the rules of conduct embodied in the Shariʿah. The scientific discoveries, the technical revolution in all its manifestations, and the economic and social transformations that have engulfed the whole world must be accommodated in a new ijtihad with a creative approach to fiqh. The Qur'an and the Prophetic Tradition have to be read alongside new developments in human knowledge and experience. But how do we exercise our intellectual faculties to resolve the current divergence between the modern world and the traditional presentation of Islamic Law and theology?

The call for a new ijtihad goes back to the nineteenth century with al-Afghānī and ʿAbdū's Salafiyyah project. The limited success of the ʿAbdū School in transforming the content of Islamic theology and law stems from the fact that they were prisoners of the old methodology. ʿAbdū's legal reforms were not sufficiently fundamental. He relied upon the views of the ancient scholars and extensively used *talfīq* or eclecticism. This was inevitable since he followed the fundamentals of *uṣūl al-fiqh*, the principles of Islamic Jurisprudence. This discipline forms the road map of Islamic Law. Unless it is altered, the jurist is bound to find himself stuck where the ancestors stopped.

Dr. Alalwani has recognized that the intellectual and social geography of the world has so changed that the old map no longer corresponds to it. His declared assessment of the Tradition, in contrast to the Qur'an, as historical rather than eternal, and his demand that the Qur'an must be held as the ultimate authority over the Tradition, is crucial for his new interpretation. More important still is his demand that the ultimate aims of the Shariʿah should be the focus of any new formulation of Shariʿah rules. The contribution of al-Shāṭibī regarding the paramount importance of the ultimate aims of the Shariʿah remained buried in his *Muwafaqāt* with little impact on the development of Islamic Law.

Although this essay deals with the minority as such, the methodology advocated here is needed everywhere and in every sphere of Islamic endeavor. The term minority is used to indicate a smaller number in relation to a greater number. The term in this context does not refer to number, but power. The community that is in control of legislation should be described here as the majority, even if it is smaller in number. The reverse is equally true: the community that is superior in number, but lacks legislative authority is, in this context, a minority. A colonial territory, for instance, has a perpetual minority status.

Is the term "Fiqh for minorities" valid as a separate discipline or is it simply an instance of the general field of Islamic Law? The author argues for the former on the basis that there are certain constraints that a minority community may experience and for which it has to find legal justification.

Dr. Alalwani calls for a collective ijtihad inviting experts from various fields of social science to play a major role in formulating new ideas and developing new perceptions. While the input of the social scientists is important I am sure that the distinguished author would welcome physical and medical scientists' contribution too. I share with him the mistrust of committees consisting exclusively of Shariʿah specialists.

Collective ijtihad is now the vogue despite the fact that it has had a limited role in the history of Islamic thought or law. I prefer contributions to be made in an atmosphere of open debate, which should lead to the adoption of the most acceptable view without delegitimizing other opinions. Our faith and society will succeed in overcoming its present crises only by giving space to divergent views to be expressed and fairly evaluated. This demands a degree of humility on the part of scholars in the tradition of Imam al-Shāfiʿī who said: "My opinion is right with the possibility of being wrong, whereas my colleague's opinion is wrong with the possibility of being right."

We have suffered in the past, and we continue to suffer from circles arrogating to themselves the exclusive right to speak for Islam. Dr. Alalwani's excellent essay pioneers the way for a meaningful approach to a new interpretation of Fiqh. He does so with the humility of the true scholar.

M. A. ZAKI BADAWI, OBE
London, January, 2003

AUTHOR'S INTRODUCTION

MUSLIM minorities did not attract as much attention in the past as they do today. Muslims were the dominant world power, feared and respected by all nations. No other power would dare attack individual Muslims or infringe upon the integrity of Islam when faced with such formidable enemies as the son of Harūn al-Rashīd, al-Muʿtaṣim[1], the Abbasid Caliph, who conquered ʿAmūriyya[2] to rescue a Muslim woman who had sought his help against the harassment of her people.

Muslims could travel freely throughout the lands of Islam. The whole world was open to them as a residence and a place of worship.[3] Allah affirms in the Qur'an: "The earth shall be inherited by my righteous servants" (*al-Anbiyā'*:105). Muslims would travel as messengers or diplomatic envoys, and as traders or itinerant Sufis. These people would be mainly visitors who would stay for short periods. Those who migrated from Muslim lands for political reasons or as dissidents – and expected to be away for a long time – would usually go to distant places where the influence of the central Muslim authority was much diluted. The more powerful and ambitious migrants of comfortably independent means would travel even to non-Muslim lands, where they would establish their own Muslim emirates, existing as Muslim oases or islands in the middle of non-Muslim oceans. Some communities, like those in the south of France, northern Italy,[4] and other places, were to survive for a long time though the expansion of Islam was halted in these territories.

Those Muslims, few as they were, lived in non-Muslim communities, where the authority was not in their hands and the laws were not based on the Shariʿah. They were mainly indigenous converts.

Eventually, they became aware of the significant difference between life in a Muslim and that in a non-Muslim community. Those who had the means migrated to Muslim lands, while others endeavored to lead as full an Islamic life as possible. They developed a distinct Islamic culture, which might, at times, cause friction with the non-Muslim host community. This because of their refusal, if that were possible, to comply with the laws and traditions that conflicted with what they had learnt of Islam. Although their new culture might indeed converge in certain aspects with the lifestyle of the host community, the degree of integration was minor and cosmetic. Friction might be provoked by the dominant majority if they attempted to eliminate the minorities' distinctive cultural and religious characteristics so as to absorb them into the non-Muslim society.

If the Muslim minorities resisted assimilation, they were likely to be subjected to persecution. They would, therefore, be helpless and lack the means to assert their existence (*al-Nisā'*: 98). They would seek fatwas from their own *ᶜulamā'* or from those outside their community, especially during the hajj season. Most of their queries would have been individual and personal. In the past, Muslim minorities were so small and isolated that they were incapable of establishing their own autonomous economic, legal or cultural organizations and institutions. Muslim jurists and *ᶜulamā'* were fully aware of a marked difference between the issues and problems of Muslim individuals and groups in a non-Muslim society, and those of a Muslim community living under Islamic law, systems, and traditions. They certainly realized the disparities between the sources of law in Muslim lands (*dār al-Islām* or *dār al-ijābah*) and those of other societies (*dār al-daᶜwah*).[5] They understood the impact of the psychological, intellectual, cultural, and juristic differences on life in both environments, thereby obliging the muftis, whether scholars or students, to investigate the evidence. They needed to contextualize that evidence in the light of the prevailing circumstances so as to issue the appropriate fatwas which could be easily and conveniently applied to their time and space, without infringing the main principles and the general aims of the Shariᶜah.

Therefore, the need for a new fiqh for minorities was not as strong in the past as it is today. This was because the "reference community" was never found outside its main country of domicile, and it had not moved to the "land of *daʿwah*" except in the limited way described above. It was a casual and transient existence that did not attract the attention of jurists to legislate and issue fatwas. It remained restricted and isolated, and its fiqh came to be known simply as the fiqh of "crises" or "emergency".[6]

PUBLIC AWARENESS OF THE SHARIʿAH

Muslims are aware that the Shariʿah laws are based on clemency and temperance rather than oppression and severity. They fully realize that the fulfillment of religious obligations is concomitant upon human ability (*al-Taghābun*: 16; *al-Baqarah*: 286). Muslims also know that the Shariʿah permits all that is clean and wholesome and forbids what is harmful, with the aim of making life easier and more convenient. It encourages and promotes good and positive conduct and forbids all that undermines society (*al-Aʿrāf*: 157).

The average Muslim understands clearly what is meant by the Qur'anic statement: "He created for you all that is on the earth" (*al-Baqarah*: 29). It confirms the use of all God's bounty with the exception of what has been specifically and categorically forbidden. Permissibility is the norm. The use of everything found in or on this earth is allowed, as long as it is clean and harmless. What is *ḥalāl* and what is *ḥarām* are clearly defined. The gray areas in between are the subject of fiqh, debate, and ijtihad.

The general and universal principles of the Qur'an created a common, widespread and accessible culture among all Muslims. With the popularity of the Qur'an and its accessibility to the general Muslim public, no matter how rudimentary their knowledge of Islam, certain standards of Islamic education and culture emerged. No other Book or religion had hitherto succeeded in achieving such a popular awareness of the law. Principles such as "religious matters known by necessity" or instinct are unique to Islamic culture.

Certain matters become common knowledge without much need for scholarship. This is unlike other religions in which every minor aspect of the liturgy and the dogma is a subject of debate and scrutiny by the clergy. They in turn possess the exclusive right and authority to judge and pronounce rulings, which are then adopted by the general public. In Islam, however, areas of specialist ijtihad are well defined and the general public is invited to offer its own input. Ordinary people can select the scholar whom they wish to follow and pick from the "common law" the reasons, terms and restrictions. They follow the scholar in adapting the facts, and there are also matters that they cannot afford to ignore.

For this reason, Muslim society has allowed the rise of the "men of the pen" in contrast to the "men of the sword." Similarly, it has no room for "priests" or "clergy" or a "grand *ᶜulamā'* board" to dominate and monopolize the sources of religious knowledge and the interpretation of religious dogma, thereby denying the rest of society access to them and preventing those who were interested from studying, analyzing and interpreting them. The idea of an élite setting itself up as a reference for religious responsibility and authority is alien to Islam. Even those who have tried to do so have failed. It is something that is rejected by the general public, not to mention the intelligentsia. The Qur'an is available to all and no one can monopolize or control access to it. Every reader of the Qur'an can learn the basics of Islam from it directly.

SHARIᶜAH AND CULTURE

There is a well-established polemical relationship between legislation, whether divine or man-made, and cultural traditions and conventions. These aspects of society influence scholars, researchers, and legislators, just as fiqh and legislation play a role in creating cultures, traditions, and conventions with a long-term impact on them. Muslim minorities live in societies in which these aspects do not stem from Islamic origins, and they themselves have no way of completely breaking away from these influences. Even if they succeed in separating themselves with respect to worship and moral conduct, they cannot do so in other general and common social transactions: education, economics, politics, the media and other public opinion-forming systems. All this contributes, in varying degrees, to the alienation of minorities from their roots and gradually weakens their bonds with them. To compensate for the loss of the old relationships, new bonds develop within the new geographical environment inhabited by the Muslim minorities.

This is true of the first generation of immigrants. Nevertheless, the old bonds may well be obliterated by the third or fourth generation and become mere bitter-sweet memories related for entertainment. Thus, the new generations may be completely assimilated into the host communities and disappear altogether, severing their links with their cultural roots, which their fathers and forefathers had made every effort to preserve.

PRESENT-DAY MUSLIM PRESENCE IN THE WEST

It is quite obvious that neither the West, especially Europe, nor the Muslims, expected to find Islam and Muslims right in the heart of Europe and the United States. These Muslims did not come as conquerors, but as immigrants, students and professionals. They were the citizens and nationals who left their Muslim lands to live in the West, forming a real, settled and permanent Muslim existence in Europe and the United States. The new immigrant communities have a very sincere wish to integrate into the host society, while preserving their religious and cultural identity. Like the rest of the population, they are quite happy and prepared to comply with and respect the law of the land, pay their taxes, assume responsibilities, and benefit from the freedom, advantages and rights provided by the law.

Until September 11, 2001, the United States considered multi-culturalism and a multi-faith society as positive contributions to its multi-lateralism in general. It was the multi-culturalism that made the United States a symbol for the whole world. It could rightly assert before all humanity and the wider world that it was the universal model for integration. This would also justify its assertion that it was the undisputed heir to Hellenism and Roman civilization: a supra-national melting-pot of cultures and races. It would rightly and deservedly become a world leader, as it has done by what has come to be known as "globalism."

The United States is to be praised for its understanding and welcoming of Islam and Muslims by all levels of society. They included some churches which offered, for very small fees, or free of charge, their premises to Muslims to use for Friday prayers and *ᶜid* days, as well as academic institutions and members of Congress from both political parties. The same can be said of certain educational institutions which welcomed Muslim members and hosted speakers and lecturers to talk about a variety of religious, cultural, historic and social issues. Some educational administrations have admitted Muslims to their governing bodies. Prison authorities have welcomed Muslim teachers and preachers to conduct prayers, teach prisoners about Islam and discuss it with them. Some of them have been appointed to well-paid positions by these authorities. They welcomed the spread of Islam through the prisons, once they witnessed its positive effects on the prisoners' behavior by persuading them to abandon drugs and avoid crime.

In 1992 the Pentagon approved the appointment of religious instructors inside the three branches of the US Armed Forces. The first minister, Chaplain Abdul-Rasheed Muhammad, was inaugurated in an official ceremony and was followed by others, comprising a final total of fourteen instructors. The number of mosques and Islamic institutions and schools markedly increased and 1997 was designated the year of the introduction of Islam and the Muslims to the United States. It was a golden opportunity that the Muslims did not successfully use to the full to present themselves, their religion, history and civilization to the nation.

Many American institutions opened their doors to Muslims. The first Muslim lady judge was appointed, and courts began consulting juristic experts when dealing with cases involving Muslim litigants.

The former First Lady employed a female Muslim assistant who wore the *ḥijāb*. A Muslim was appointed to a senior position at the White House, while the State Department has been inquiring into the appointment of Muslims as possible future ambassadors. The first Muslim American ambassador was appointed to Fiji. The Pentagon agreed to modify uniforms for female Muslim officers and privates to include a headscarf worn under the cap. All civilian and military government employees were encouraged to read and learn about Islam before going to Muslim countries so as to avoid offending local sensibilities or cultural traditions and thus provoking a negative reaction toward the United States and its citizens. These efforts have led to a good understanding of Islam and Muslims. Some people have been inspired to convert to Islam or, at least, to respect it and its followers, to be ready to appreciate their cause and, in certain cases, to empathize with it.

Cases have been brought before the courts against pressure on Muslim women to remove the *ḥijāb* or the headcover, all of which were resolved in favor of the Muslim women. Muslim men and women are now clearly visible with their distinctive dress, raising public awareness and interest in their religion, history and culture. They highlight the positive aspects of Islam that can be passed on to this country, especially in family life, and they practice what I refer to as "the silent *daʿwah*."*

---

*With large Muslim populations in France, Germany, Sweden and the UK, amongst others, Muslims have become part of the fabric of European life. In Britain, for example, Muslims are free to practice their religion fully and the existence of more than a 1000 mosques is testament to this freedom. Community relations between Muslims and non-Muslims in recent times have been on the whole good. However, prejudice and Islamophobia still exist. The Muslim community welcomed the fact that it was the British government itself which commissioned a report to look into anti-Muslim discrimination and prejudice. The report, entitled *Islamophobia, A Challenge for Us All* (1998) was the first serious attempt to look at the topic and was used widely by Muslims and non-Muslims. In the education sector, after much campaigning, there is now some state provision of schools with a wholly Islamic ethos. Due to the acceptance of European legislation which affords protection to minorities, inroads have been made in securing the rights of Muslims to

SEPTEMBER 11TH: THE AFTERMATH

The shattering events of September 11 have left everyone in a state of shock. Since then, Muslims and Americans have woken up to a new reality, the like of which has never been known before. Since then, the need has arisen, as never before, for a new fiqh dealing with the question of Muslim minorities in the West in particular.

Large numbers of non-Muslim Americans from all strata of society have turned toward learning about Islam from its original sources and from its followers, rather than from others. Books and publications on Islam in general, or on certain aspects of its origins, history, culture or civilization, have been sold out and public libraries have ordered extra copies to lend to readers. Inevitably, such a phenomenal interest has created some misunderstanding. Certain naïve individuals thought that it was due to a desire to convert to Islam or to seek an alternative religious faith. However, it was no more than an effort to resist ignorance and a genuine urge to learn.

Numerous churches, universities, and research and study institutions have embarked on inviting imams, professors and lecturers to speak on Islam and expound its principles, sources, relationship to other religions and its effect on its followers. In addition, speakers are invited to answer questions that are raised by many Americans about Islam, especially those debated in the media relating to the link between Islamic beliefs and extremism. People wish to know if Prophet Muhammad (ṢAAS)[7] taught his followers to be extremist and whether he ordered them to kill their opponents or those who

---

practice Islam freely. Legislation has been passed which outlaws discrimination against Muslims (and those of other faiths) in the workplace. Muslims are also involving themselves in the wider society. Muslim periodicals such as *Emel*, and prominent Muslim journalists and broadcasters have shown how far Muslims have progressed. In the field of politics, the situation is contrasted with that of America, where there are no Muslim Senators. In Britain Muslim peers have been appointed to the House of Lords, and Muslims have been elected as members of parliament showing how far Muslims have become part and parcel of British life, and by extension the rest of Europe. [Editors].

did not believe in Islam. What is the Islamic view of the freedom of the human being? Does Islam exclude freedom of religion? Some people cite extracts from the Qur'an, such as verses 5 of *al-Tawbah* or 191–194 of *al-Baqarah*, which they may have heard or read out of context. These misconceptions can cause people to judge Islam to be a militant faith, ever advocating fighting, war, and the use of duress to coerce others,* kill them or force them to pay protection money. Some have cited the Prophet's battles against his enemies as proof of Islam's militancy.

Nor has all this been enough to satisfy Islam's detractors. Many of them have reverted to established works and references in fiqh and other Islamic sciences to randomly select passages, terms and statements and interrogate Muslim imams and workers about them. However, many of the people questioned usually have only a rudimentary knowledge of Islam, and so they tend to apologize for those statements and dismiss them as ancient and irrelevant. They give way to strange paradoxical feelings of inferiority. However these misconceptions and misunderstandings and certain stereotypes continue to be raised. Some of these are:

- Islam divides the world into the "land of Islam" and the "land of war." Does this not mean that Muslims are in a state of continual war with the rest of the world? Does it not give Muslims the right to fight the followers of any other religion whenever they wish and whenever they find themselves strong enough to declare war on others? Were the events of September 11 a result of the Muslims' belief that Americans are infidels and that their country is a "land of war?"

---

*See forthcoming book by Dr. Taha Jabir Alalwani, *Apostasy in Islam: A Historical and Scriptural Analysis* (2010). This work examines in careful detail the arguments put forward by proponents of the death penalty arguing that evidence from the Qur'an and the Sunnah does not support capital punishment for the sin of *riddah* but in contrast promotes freedom of belief including the act of exiting the faith. As long as one's apostasy has not been accompanied by anything else that would be deemed a criminal act, it remains a matter strictly between God and the individual. [Editors].

- What about *jizyah*, (the "poll tax") which Muslims insist that Jews and Christians pay with humiliation. It is a degrading tax that infringes upon people's rights, and the freedom to choose the faith in which they believe?

- How about coercing and forcing Muslims who convert to other religions to reconvert to Islam on pain of the death penalty? Is this not the kind of compulsion that you assert is rejected by your faith?

- What about the rights of women whom Muslims believe to be of inferior minds and lesser religious conviction? A woman's testimony, according to your faith, counts as half of that of a man. What about the right to detain your women in the home, and the right of the man to marry four wives, whereas a woman can have only one husband, whom she has to serve and obey? A woman cannot disobey her husband's wishes or separate from him because he alone has the right to end the marriage. What about *ḥijāb*? Do you not see that imposing it on women is a form of humiliation and undermines your trust in them? Does this not confirm the belief that a woman is a second-class citizen who exists solely for the satisfaction of man's sexual desires, bearing and looking after his children, and taking care of his home? Nevertheless, the man is still considered superior to the woman and he has the last word on whether to keep or divorce her. Moreover, a woman's share of an inheritance is half that of a man. How about depriving women and beating them if they disobey their men?[8]

- What about the amputation of a hand for theft, the stoning to death for adultery, and the killing of homosexuals, using the vilest means such as burning them to death at the stake or throwing them from a great height?

- Why are vile dictatorship, human rights abuses, disease, backwardness, prejudice, and extremism so rife in your countries? Why have all the efforts of development and modernization in your countries failed so miserably? Is not Islam the cause of your backwardness, just as Christianity was the cause of our progress, once we had put it in its rightful place? Why have you failed in adopting democracy? Is this not evidence that the teachings of Islam encourage oppression, dictatorship, class differences, and other similar afflictions?

- Why does Islam teach you that killing yourselves in order to kill civilians in Palestine and New York will lead you to Paradise?

Such misconceptions, questions, queries and stereotypes need to be intelligently and correctly approached and responded to. They can no longer be dismissed or brushed under the carpet.

LEGAL AND RELIGIOUS FRAMEWORK

DEFINITIONS

Fiqh

The current usage of the term fiqh, Islamic jurisprudence, was not common in the early days of Islam. The term more widely used then was *fahm*, or "comprehension" of the pre-ordained purpose and wisdom of the command of God. In more intricate issues that required closer examination, some would use instead the term fiqh, or "understanding." In *al-Muqqadimah*, Ibn Khaldūn says:

> Fiqh is the knowledge of God's rules, *aḥkām*, regarding the behavior and actions of adult individuals, be they obligatory, forbidden, recommended, abhorrent or permissible. These rules are received from the Qur'an and the Sunnah and the means God has established to ascertain them. The formulation and articulation of these rules, using those means, is what is referred to as fiqh.[9]

The term *fuqahā'*, jurists or fiqh practitioners, was not common in those days either. To distinguish them from their unlearned or illiterate contemporaries, the Prophet's Companions who devoted themselves to deduction and the reasoning of religious rules were known as "students" or "readers." Ibn Khaldūn says:

> Then the lands of Islam expanded and illiteracy among the Arabs receded due to the spread of literacy. The practice of deduction took hold, fiqh flourished and became a vocation and a science. Thus, "readers" and "students" became jurists, or *fuqahā'*.[10]

Minorities

The term "minorities" is a political one that has come into use in contemporary international convention. It refers to a group or groups of state subjects of a racial, lingual or religious affiliation different from that of the majority population.

The demands of minorities often include those of the equality of civil and political rights, the recognition of the right to be different and distinctive in beliefs, values and personal status as well as such other matters that do not infringe on the overall framework they share with the rest of society. Leaders often emerge amongst minorities to articulate and express the particular features and aspirations of their group through the following ways:

- The education of the minority group in its history and origins, and the definition of its ethnic characteristics and *raison d'etre*, in order to answer such questions as: "Who are we?" and "What do we want?"
- The forging of ties between minority members.
- The promotion of an educated élite to represent the minority's distinctive culture and traditions.
- The establishment and promotion of initiatives to secure the livelihood and social welfare of the group's members following the successful example of Jewish minorities.

A "Fiqh for Minorities"

The discussion of a "fiqh for minorities" raises a number of questions:

- Under what discipline should this fiqh be placed?
- What subjects of the social sciences does it relate to, and how far does it interact with other disciplines?
- How did it come to be known as the "fiqh for minorities" and how accurate is this terminology?

- What approach should be adopted when dealing with issues arising from large concentrations of Muslims living outside the geographical and historical Islamic domain?

The "fiqh for minorities" cannot be included under fiqh as it is understood today, i.e. the fiqh of minor issues. Rather, it ought to come under the science of fiqh in its general sense, which covers all theological and practical branches of Islamic law and jurisprudence. This would be in line with the meaning of fiqh used by the Prophet in the hadith: "He to whom God wishes good, He makes him articulate in the religion."[11] Imam Abū Ḥanīfah referred to this knowledge as the "greater fiqh," or macro-fiqh, a phrase which he chose as the title of his great work on the subject.

For this reason, we believe it is more appropriate to categorize the "fiqh for minorities" under fiqh in the macro, or general, sense to avoid the creation of a legislative or fiqh vacuum.

"Fiqh for minorities" is a specific discipline which takes into account the relationship between the religious ruling and the conditions of the community and the location where it exists. It is a fiqh that applies to a specific group of people living under particular conditions with special needs that may not be appropriate for other communities. Besides religious knowledge, practitioners of this fiqh will need a wider acquaintance with several social sciences disciplines, especially sociology, economics, political science and international relations.

The term "fiqh for minorities" is, therefore, a precise definition, acceptable from both a religious as well as a conventional point of view. It is not meant to give minorities privileges or concessions not available to Muslim majorities. On the contrary, it aims to project minorities as representative models or examples of Muslim society in countries in which they live. It is the fiqh of model communities, élites and, a rigorous rather than frivolous or concessionary, approach. Based on the rules and fundamentals of this fiqh, a number of parameters have been identified which may define our method in responding to questions from minority members. The main features of these parameters will be elaborated later in this discussion.

REDEFINING THE QUESTION

When a question relating to minorities is raised, the contemporary fiqh practitioner or mufti will need to understand that he is dealing with a situation beyond the simplistic one of an inquirer unable to obtain an Islamic ruling on a problem he is facing and a scholar who sees his duty as nothing more than giving a fatwa. This is an extremely unscientific approach, inherited from an era when traditional adherence to established doctrine, *taqlīd*, was reinforced by illiterate members of society who found it easier to follow and imitate their teachers and predecessors.

Today, a more logical and scientific approach is required, one that delves deeply into the background of both the query and the inquirer, as well as pays close attention to the underlying social factors that caused the question to be raised. Is the form in which the question has been worded acceptable, or should it be modified and represented as an issue of fiqh to be treated within a comprehensive context that brings into play major Shariʿah rules, guiding Qur'anic principles, higher governing values, and the essential objectives of Islamic law?

We may be able to appreciate more deeply the Qur'anic advice not to raise questions whose answers could lead to serious social problems, for these questions are considered the result of negative factors which would only be reinforced should the answers be provided. The Qur'an has imparted to us a methodical approach by which issues are broken down and questions reconstructed before they are answered. For example: "They ask you about the new moons. Say: 'New moons are means people use for measuring time, and for pilgrimage'" (*al-Baqarah*: 189). The question, as originally expressed by the Jews of Madinah, was concerned with the physical aspects of the phases of the moon and why they occurred. However, in the Qur'an it was reconstructed to deal with the functions of the moon, linking its apparent size and orbit with the determination of information such as times and dates constantly sought by human-kind.

The whole question then becomes an exercise in education on several levels. Firstly, to teach people how to phrase questions accurately so as to elicit appropriate and correct answers. Secondly, to highlight all the elements that shapes the question, eliminating those hidden in the inquirer's mind that can be done away with or ignored. Inquirers often have different intentions and unless the respondent is aware of this fact, he can easily be diverted into giving the wrong response. Inquiries arise for a variety of reasons: there are questions that seek knowledge or information; there are affirmative questions; rhetorical questions; loaded questions that refute a statement or contradict it; leading questions aimed at exposing the ignorance of the respondent, and so on. Thirdly, to prepare the inquirer for receiving the appropriate answer. This approach is evident in the majority of cases where direct inquiries are raised in the Qur'an (*al-Isrā'*: 85, *al-Kahf*: 83, and so on). Inquiry has its own manners that must be observed by both the inquirer and the respondent.

Accordingly, one can appreciate the Prophet's dislike of idle talk and of asking too many questions, or badly phrased ones, that might result in giving the wrong ruling or judgement.

One may then ask: can Muslim minorities participate in the political life of a host country where the non-Muslims form a majority and where the political system is non-Islamic? An intelligent jurist, appreciating the universality of Islam, the role of the Muslim community in the world and the necessary interaction between cultures and civilizations in contemporary international life would decline to respond to a question formulated in this manner. He would change its tone from a negative to a positive one, based on his knowledge of Islam's universal aims and the unique characteristics of both the faith and the Muslim community. Rephrased and restructured, the question would then become: What is Islam's view regarding a group of Muslims who find themselves living among a non-Muslim majority whose system of government allows them to observe and exercise all Islamic obligations that do not threaten public order? Furthermore, the system allows members of the Muslim minority to attain public office, influence policy, assume leadership positions, propagate their beliefs and set up useful social institutions. Should such a minority relinquish these rights and decline these opportunities for fear of assimilation into the non-Muslim majority or of being influenced by them?

When put this way, the question still satisfies the objectives of the original, but reflects a sense of responsibility, steering the response towards a more constructive direction. Instead of seeking a license to justify a negative situation, the debate turns to dealing with obligations, positive action and constructive roles.

THE NEED FOR SPECIALIST IJTIHAD IN THE FORMULATION OF A FIQH FOR MINORITIES

In recent decades, Muslims have settled in many countries outside Islam's historic and geographic sphere. Within these countries, which have witnessed a growth in the spread of Islam, Muslims are having to face new situations that raise many issues far beyond the limited personal ones such as *ḥalāl* food, the sighting of the new moon, or marriage to non-Muslim women. The debate has now turned to greater and much more profound issues relating to Muslim identity, the role of Muslims in their new homeland, their relationship to the world Muslim community, the future of Islam outside its present borders and how it may go forward to establish its universality in all parts of the globe.

Some may have tried to view these issues as arising out of expediency or the product of exceptional circumstances, forgetting that this approach is extremely narrow and limited. It cannot deal with problems relating to the building of a strong minority. Besides, it clearly has many repercussions harmful to the Muslim psyche and character in general. No wonder Muslims find themselves in a sea of confusion. Faced as they are with differences in opinion among jurists: some – to varying degrees of strictness – citing differences between life in Muslim and non-Muslim societies (the so-called *dār al-Islām* and *dār al-ḥarb*), and others comparing the present with the past and ignoring the huge social and historic changes that have occurred. This confusion and disarray has forced Muslims into isolation and restricted their contribution. It has disrupted Muslim life and kept it backward. Above all, it has portrayed the Islamic faith as being incapable of facing and resolving the important issues of the age such as progress and development.

The problems of Muslim minorities can only be tackled with a fresh juristic vision, based on the principles, objectives and higher values of the Qur'an in conjunction with the aims of the Shari^c^ah. A new methodology for replicating the Prophet's example is needed in order to make his way clearer and more accessible to everyone at all times.

WHAT CAN BE LEARNED FROM THE INHERITED FIQH?

Though varied and rich, the volume of theoretical fiqh bequeathed to us dealing with relations between Muslims and non-Muslims is part of its own time and space and none of it can be applied to other substantially different situations. It can only be considered as a precedent to be examined, noted, and studied in order to discern the principles upon which it was based and which guided our predecessors to produce it. This wealth of jurisprudence is of value to today's jurists to provide them with the skills and methods to respond to the needs of the times. The aim should not be to apply the old fatwas literally, but to use them as a guide, learning how to obtain the original principles, the "roots" or *uṣūl*, from which earlier jurists derived and articulated them.

Our pioneering jurists bequeathed to us a golden rule which states: the changing of rulings should not be censured by the change of time. Many jurists, such as Imam al-Shāfiʿī and others, were flexible with certain rulings and opinions, changing them according to the realities of a particular situation or specific reason which arose as they moved from one country to another, or when certain conditions pertaining to the earlier situation had changed, or simply because times had changed. Several innovative jurists indicated that their differences with their own teachers over certain issues were simply due to "the changing of times and situations, rather than to new evidence or reasoning."

The Prophet also set a good precedent when he advised against visiting graveyards but later permitted it saying: "Visit them because they remind you of the hereafter."[12] The same flexibility was also applied to the storing of meat and many other similar instances.[13]

The Prophet's Companions adopted the same approach and never flinched from amending or changing their views and rulings whenever they found reason or justification for so doing, due to changes of time or space. Many of the rulings advanced by the four successors of the Prophet included minor as well as major amendments to rulings applied during his lifetime, while some were totally new. (See endnote 14 for some examples.)[14]

Muslims of the second generation followed a similar practice, deviating in their rulings over certain issues from the views of their predecessors. (See endnote 15 for some examples.)[15]

A study of cases dealt with by the Prophet's contemporaries and their followers clearly shows that they had understood very well the specific purpose, wisdom, reasons and causes underlying the Shariʿah. The study, interpretation, comprehension and application of all religious text should take place within the framework of the purposes and reasons of the Shariʿah and the underlying wisdom. Insistence on mere linguistic or literal interpretation would not relieve jurists from their responsibility until the ultimate objectives of the Shariʿah are served. Rigid or dogmatic attitudes and semantics can only lead to a fiqh similar to that of the Israelites in their argument with Moses (AS)[16] over the sacrificial cow, as related in the Qur'an (2:67–71). The need to go beyond the limited fiqh inherited from past generations remains strong for several reasons, some of which relate to methodology and others to the ultimate objectives (*maqāṣid*) of the Islamic Shariʿah.

REASONS FOR A NEW METHODOLOGY

1. Some earlier jurists did not classify the sources of Islamic law in a precise way, one that would facilitate the deduction of rulings for contemporary issues. Such a system of classification would

consider the Qur'an as the ultimate and overriding source of all legislation, the absolute criterion and the final reference. It is immutable and incontrovertible. In second place would come the Sunnah of the Prophet as a complementary and explanatory reference, expanding, elaborating and extending the Qur'anic rulings and principles.

2. Most jurists overlooked the universality of Islam as a defining factor in their rationalization and analysis of relations between Muslims and non-Muslims. Their work reflects a certain degree of introversion, incompatible with the universality of Islam's eternal message. There has also been excessive preoccupation with parochial factors of geography and society, strongly associating Islam with the social and geographic environment.

3. The thinking of Muslim jurists with respect to the geo-political world map of the time was influenced by contemporaneous historic convention. They overlooked the Qur'anic concept of the world and human geography and their works have tended to be localized and provincial.

4. The higher values, principles and objectives of Islamic legislation were obscured, reinforcing a partial, fractional and personalized image of fiqh. Imam al-Ghazālī described fiqh as "a minor science."

REASONS FOR A CLEAR OBJECTIVE

1. In the early days following the time of the Prophet, Muslims were not used to seeking justice or refuge in non-Muslim lands. The land of Islam was one, sovereign and secure, with no borders to divide it. Inhabitants were free to roam from one part of the vast empire to the other without any feelings of alienation, estrangement or inferiority.

2. "Citizenship," as the concept is understood today, was unknown during the heyday of Islamic fiqh. Instead, there was

cultural and political affiliation often based on ideological and traditional loyalties. Inter-religious and cultural interaction were undertaken with reserve and caution, mixed with varying degrees of tolerance. Europe had the Spanish Inquisition while Muslims treated non-Muslims as *ahl al-dhimmah.* In other words, non-Muslim citizens, most notably Jews and Christians, could enjoy protection and safety while living in a Muslim state.

3. There were no established criteria, such as birth, domicile or marriage, for gaining citizenship in another country. Common beliefs and culture were sufficient to confer "citizenship" on new arrivals who would otherwise remain as outsiders or foreign to the indigenous society.

4. The ancient world had no concept or experience of international law or diplomatic conventions obliging host countries to protect immigrants or mete out to them equal treatment, except in certain distinguishing matters.

5. The rationale of power was reigning supreme in relations among ancient empires, including the Muslim empire. Each considered the other as enemy territory which it had the right to overrun and annex, in full or in part. Empires knew no frontiers and their armies stopped advancing only when the terrain prevented them.

6. Our predecessors did not experience the closely-connected world we live in today and its interacting cultures and global-village atmosphere. Their world was made up of separate "islands," with limited cohabitation or understanding of one another. The "fiqh of conflict" was then prevalent, dictated by the times, but what is needed today is a fiqh of "coexistence" which suits our world in spirit as well as in form.

7. Some jurists express in their fatwas a kind of resistance or reaction to a particular social context that is different from ours of today.

A good example of this is Ibn Taymiyyah's views on the need for Muslims to be different from Jewish, Christian or other non-Muslim groups and his opposition to enlisting their help.[17] One could also cite the early-twentieth-century fatwa of the Algerian *ʿulamā'* prohibiting taking up French citizenship. These and other similar opinions stem from a "culture of conflict" which Muslim minorities today can better do without.

TOWARDS A FOUNDATION FOR A FIQH FOR MINORITIES

In this monograph, we try to introduce a set of methodological principles which we consider should be taken into account by students of fiqh for minorities. Like all fiqh, this special discipline requires rules and principles of its own.

The science of principles of fiqh, or *uṣūl al-fiqh*, is one of the most noble of the theoretical sciences to have been formulated by our pioneering scholars. Imam al-Ghazālī described it well when he wrote: "It is a science that combines reason with oral tradition, opinion with religious text, producing an elegant synthesis of both."[18]

However, when this science first emerged, practitioners applied it as a tool for settling on-going debates between advocates of hadith and those of reason. From these beginnings, it grew and developed, in the process spilling over into other theoretical as well as practical Islamic sciences in the hope that it might bring these two camps together. Although it was also influenced by other sciences, it continued to retain its original structure, as envisaged by pioneering scholars such as Imam al-Shāfiʿī and others. We have compiled a concise history of the development and codification of this science since the publication of al-Shāfiʿī's *al-Risālah* up to the present.[19] The main conclusion of this research is that, despite the passing of centuries, the subject has not developed a great deal. Except in works of collation, abridgment, interpretation and commentary, there has hardly been any significant new contribution. As mentioned above Imam al-Ghazālī classified it as a minor science.

The main contribution worth mentioning here is that of Imam al-Shāṭibī who developed some of the ideas of Imam al-Ḥaramayn, al-Ghazālī and others relating to the objectives (*maqāṣid*) of Shariʿah. His contribution stands as a landmark in the evolution of the theory of fiqh. Modern scholars such as Shaykh al-Ṭāhir ibn ʿĀshūr,[20] ʿAllāl al-Fāsī,[21] Aḥmad al-Raysūnī,[22] and Yūsuf al-ʿĀlim[23] developed these objectives of Shariʿah even further to form a science in its own right (*maqāṣid al-sharīʿah*), almost independent from *uṣūl al-fiqh*. One hopes, however, that such a separation does not take place in our case, as it did to earlier disciplines such as "General Rules of Fiqh," "Extraction of Secondary Rules from Primary Rules," and "Debate and Disagreement." If this were to happen today, we fear that the science of fiqh would revert to stagnation and become yet again a mere collection of philosophical and polemic rules or linguistic and intellectual arguments, or a set of works borrowed from Qur'anic and hadith sciences. As such, it would no longer be an area for innovation or development but a selection of treatises. The vital science which Muṣṭafā ʿAbd al-Rāziq called "Islamic Philosophy"[24] must be reviewed and researched thoroughly in order for it to be forever open and a part of the overall system of Islamic knowledge. It should continue to play its role as laid down by the pioneering scholars who intended it to be the science for new intellectual and juristic innovators and for developing juristic talent that would conform with the Qur'anic approach.

In defining the fiqh for minorities, we have attempted to highlight the most important aspects of fiqh theory and its methodological limitations which require special attention, without overlooking our rich fiqh legacy, upon which we aim to build and develop further. The theory of the fiqh for minorities does not ignore the reasoning of the science of fiqh or the rules of extrapolation. It is exercised within the established rules of ijtihad, or those of interpretative analysis. What we aim to do is deploy the techniques and tools of ijtihad in a way that is compatible with our time and the new explosion in knowledge, the sciences and means of learning, and restore the role of Shariʿah in modern life. There is no doubt that the role of ijtihad is to regulate and guide man's actions to accomplish his role as the vicegerent of God on earth, as God intended. If this is achieved, the end will be positive and conducive to man receiving the appropriate reward.

Conflict between the means and the ends shall render the whole exercise futile and those who engage in it shall be penalized accordingly. God says in the Qur'an: "And then We shall turn to what they [the evil-doers] had done and render it scattered dust" (*al-Furqān*: 23). Whenever human actions overshoot the desired objective, they become counter-productive and undermine the purpose of man's role in the world. Failure, humiliation and punishment will be the consequences.

The pivotal issue here, then, is the nature, value, quality and purpose of man's actions. This is the fundamental objective of legislation now and in the past, divine or man-made. All divine doctrines were aimed at guiding man's actions to fulfill the purpose of his being which is to serve God in the widest possible sense of the word. Such fulfillment shall be reflected in life in the form of prosperity and advancement, and in the human heart as pure monotheism, *tawḥīd*, and as good and constructive behavior.

The whole controversy over prophethood and man's need for it, the human mind and its powers and limitations, finite text and infinite events, is related to a central fact. This may be summarized as follows: Is the human mind independently capable of evaluating human behavior, or should this be a function of divine Revelation alone? Must the two act together in this context in order to identify the relationship between human behavior and God's purpose behind creation? Islam's final answer is that the two must work jointly in the evaluation process, because they are complementary and mutually indispensable. The following should be taken into consideration in the process of formulating a fiqh for minorities:

1. Ijtihad is an extremely vital function and a distinctive feature of the Muslim Ummah (community). It is not known to exist in most religious systems because, in earlier religions, prophetic teachings constituted the highest and most noble repository of

knowledge and wisdom and could only be received directly from God Almighty by the prophets who passed them on to their immediate disciples and priests who possessed certain qualifications not conferred upon ordinary people.

Furthermore, earlier religious teachings to which people had to submit tended to be severe and austere. They were supported by physical miracles as proof and demanded responses that did not require the use of cause-and-effect reasoning.

2. Islam is the first religion to recognize unconditionally the role of the human mind in the evaluation and judgement of human behavior. In fact, it insists on that role, believing that while the origin of the Shariʿah is divine, its application in the real world of human behavior is human. God says: "For each of you We have ordained a system of laws and assigned a path" (*al-Mā'idah*: 48).

3. Islam made ijtihad an intellectual state of mind that inspires man to think systematically and according to specific rational methods, and not simply as a dogmatic activity constrained within the mere formulation of rules and fatwas.

4. Many people these days are advocating ijtihad; the secularists are using it as a pretext to temper and distort the rules of Shariʿah, and the loyalists to forge a link between the past and the present and revive the Shariʿah. What is urgently needed today is the ijtihad that prepares Islam and Muslims for a global role in the future.

In order to establish the foundations of this kind of ijtihad, it will be necessary to recall certain important rules and test their validity on issues relating to minorities. If these are found to be conducive and encouraging, they can be tested in other areas; otherwise, they may be put aside for future research.

1. Our understanding of religion and religious practice should, in the first instance, be based on the study of divine revelation on

the one hand, and the real dynamic world on the other. The Qur'an guides us to the marvels and secrets of the physical world while reflection on the real world leads us back to understanding the Qur'an. We must appreciate how the two interact, contrast and complement each other.

This is what we refer to as the "combined reading": a reading of Revelation for an understanding of the physical world and its laws and principles, and a reading of the physical world to appreciate and recognize the value of Revelation. The purpose of reading revelation is to apply the general "key principles" to specific situations and link the absolute to the relative, as far as our capabilities allow. The reader in all cases is man, God's vicegerent on earth, guided by his strong faith in Revelation and his understanding of it on the one hand, and his appreciation of the laws and behavior of the physical world on the other.[25]

When Imam ʿAlī (RAA)[26] was confronted by the slogan: "No rule but God's rule," he responded by saying: "The Qur'an is a book that speaks only through the mouths of men." This is a fundamental philosophical observation since, in the absence of proper methodology, the meaning and implication of revealed text is determined and influenced by human culture, expertise, knowledge, and experience. This methodology, the "combined reading" in this context, does not come into its own until the metaphysical dimension of life is brought into the fore. Thus, the body of knowledge which is beyond human perception, what the Qur'an refers to as *ghayb*, is translated into laws and principles to be studied and debated among scientists rigorously and objectively. This is done once we differentiate between what is relatively beyond our perception as human beings, which gradually unfolds with time, and what is absolutely out of the bounds of human knowledge. In this way, we are able to identify from the Qur'an itself workable and practical methodologies for such concepts as the "counter accident" and "counter absurd" theories and the theory of "normism," and the supremacy of the Qur'an which makes the Sunnah of the Prophet a practical interpretation of the Qur'an without any conflict or contradiction in the authority of the two sources.

Once the process of the "combined reading" is underway, we shall find that the most noble values that the two "readings" highlight are the following: monotheism (*tawḥīd*); purification (*tazkiyah*); and civilization (*ʿumrān*). *Tawḥīd* is the belief in the absolute and pure Oneness of God Almighty as the Creator, Maker and Everlasting Lord. The second value, *tazkiyah*, relates to man as God's vicegerent on earth, entrusted by and accountable to Him, charged with building and developing the world. He can only achieve this through self-purification. *ʿUmrān* is taken to mean the cultivation and development of the world as the arena harnessed for discharging man's mission and the crucible for his trials, accountability and development.

These values are, in fact, ends in themselves, reflecting God's purpose behind the creation of the world, which was not pointless, and the creation of man, which was not in vain, and His admonition not to corrupt the earth. These three values, or objectives, come under the heading of "worship," and it has been necessary to understand and highlight them from the outset as the criteria by which human behavior is judged. Duties and obligations rest on these values and stem from them. They feature very prominently in understanding the Sunnah as well as the work of the Companions and the rightly-guided Caliphs, especially that of Abū Bakr and ʿUmar. There are countless examples to show how, in their interpretations and fatwas, they had always referred to the main and fundamental principles, fully cognizant of the higher values and objectives of Islam, from which they extracted secondary and specific rulings. This is also frequently found in the fatwas of Imam ʿAlī, and some of ʿUthmān's. It is clear in all their opinions and interpretations that have reached us. It can also be observed in the fiqh of the following generation who learnt from them and their contemporaries.

In defining fiqh terms and the codification of the fiqh literature, however, later generations of jurists were bogged down in dogma and terminology, and were influenced by the translated works of philosophy and logic. They began to borrow the terms of those works in order to classify duties and obligations as mandatory, obligatory, recommended, preferred, prohibited or forbidden; or otherwise unconditionally permissible. This, in order to relate these terms to the concepts of reward and punishment, praise and rejection, and so on. Thus a hiatus was created within the science of fiqh where the fundamental purpose of its rulings was lost until they re-emerged in the works of al-Shāṭibī. The higher purposes of religion were limited to the immediate objectives of adult humans and they appeared to be divorced from "interests," (*maṣāliḥ*) which is not the case.

Hence the need to go back to the very beginning and start the evaluation of human activity with the higher governing values and purposes and then go on to conferring the prescription: "do" or "don't", and so on. We must view rational issues and philosophical terms as secondary, for the risk of overlooking or discarding some of these terms is far less serious than disregarding the higher governing values and purposes.

2. On another score, we must consider the levels of purpose with reference to responsible adults apropos of "expediency," "priority" and "embellishment," which should be linked to the three higher values: *tawḥīd*, *tazkiyah* and *ᶜumrān*. This will open wide the doors for jurists who are capable of including all new situations under these levels, as was done by Shaykh Ibn ᶜĀshūr who listed freedom as one of the main purposes of Shariᶜah. So did Shaykh Muhammad al-Ghazālī who included equality and human rights among its purposes. There are other issues that need to be included among the needs and priorities of the Muslim community and these should be accommodated accordingly.

3. Jurists have identified certain questions under the heading: "Issues common to the Qur'an and the Sunnah," and although they standardized their terms, they are, in fact, not the same. The Qur'anic text is the direct word of God Almighty, the eternal and absolute miracle. It is a sacred text that cannot be allegorically read or interpreted. It was undoubtedly revealed in the language of Prophet Muhammad, but the text bears certain meanings when it is pronounced by God Almighty and a different one when uttered by the Prophet, and yet a third when recited by ordinary human mortals.

For this reason, the words of God and the words of His Prophet must never be unconditionally or unreservedly equated. The important minute differences in nuance between the Qur'an and the Sunnah do not allow such absolute equality, despite the fact that both of them originate from one and the same source. The tendency to equate between the Qur'an and the Sunnah has, at times, led to confusion in understanding the true relationship between the two sources. For, although they are not the same, contradiction or conflict between them cannot be possible. The Qur'an is the source that sets the rules, values and standards which the Sunnah explains and elaborates further. The Qur'an, in fact, endorses and legitimizes the other available sources, including the Sunnah, and supersedes them. The Sunnah revolves around the Qur'an and is closely tied up with it, but never surpasses or overrules it. The confusion in defining the relationship between the Qur'an and the Sunnah has produced a number of absurd notions such as: the Qur'an and the Sunnah mutually annul or cancel each other; the Sunnah is the judge of the Qur'an; the Qur'an is far more dependent on the Sunnah than the other way round. These claims made the relationship between the Qur'an and the Sunnah one of precise logic, of either definite or speculative nature, which is contrary to the Qur'anic description of the relationship. In the Qur'an, we read: "We have revealed to you the Qur'an, so that you may make clear to people what has been revealed to them, and that they may reflect" (*al-Naḥl*: 44); "We have revealed to you the Book so that you may clarify for them what they had disputed over, and as a guide and a mercy for true believers" (*al-Naḥl*: 64); and "We have revealed to you the Book that explains everything and which is a guide and a mercy and good news for those who surrender themselves to God" (*al-Naḥl*: 89).

We therefore call for a review of the relationship between the Qur'an and the Sunnah. The Qur'an must be freed of many of the allegations surrounding it. Its language should be understood outside the lexicon of pre-Islamic Arabic and according to its own grammar, just as its style and prose were their own standard. The Qur'an is simple and accessible to all serious students. The fact that it can have different interpretations is an aspect of its miraculous nature and a rich advantage. Humanity is in greater need of the Qur'an's guidance than ever before; a book which encompasses all time and space and the nature of man. It deals with all issues and offers solutions and answers to all questions.

As for sources other than the Qur'an and the Sunnah, known as secondary or minor sources and estimated to be around forty-seven in number, there is no universal agreement; some of them can be classified under methodology, while others are concerned with interpretation, comprehension and elaboration. They are used in as far as they support and elucidate the Qur'an and its objectives and values.

METHODOLOGICAL PRINCIPLES FOR THE STUDY OF THE QUR'AN

There is a need to propose and develop principles to assist in revealing more of the purposes of the Qur'an. This should, in turn, help in building up fiqh rules for minorities as well as majorities. Here are some suggested principles:

1. Unveiling the structural unity of the Qur'an by reading it in contrast to the physical universe and its movement. The Sunnah of the infallible Prophet is viewed as the practical example and an interpretation of the Qur'an's values in the real world. The Sunnah should also be viewed as an integrated structure in its own right, closely linked to the Qur'an as an elaboration of its values for relative specific situations.

2. Acknowledging the supremacy and precedence of the Qur'an as the judge over all else, including the sayings and actions of the Prophet. Once the Qur'an establishes a certain principle, such as tolerance and justice in dealing with non-Muslims, the ruling of the Qur'an takes precedence. The sayings and actions of the Prophet, in this case, should, if possible, be interpreted to conform to the principle established by the Qur'an and be subservient to it. One of the examples in this case is the interpretation of a hadith regarding not to return the greetings of a non-Muslim with a better greeting which does not seem to conform to the teachings of the Qur'an.

3. Recalling that the Qur'an has revived the legacy of earlier prophets. It verifies, evaluates, and expurgates this legacy of all distortions, and then represents it in a purified form in order to standardize human references. This is how the Qur'an has embraced the legacy of previous prophets and taken supremacy over it.

4. Reflecting on the purpose of the Qur'an in linking the reality of human life with that which is beyond human perception, or *ghayb*, and discrediting the notion of randomness or coincidence. This facilitates an understanding of the relationship between the seen and the unseen worlds, the knowable and the unknowable; between the absolute text of the Qur'an and the real human condition. It reveals part of the delicate distinction between man's humanity and individuality. As an individual, man is a relative being, but his humanity makes him a universal and an absolute one.

5. Recalling the importance of the factors of time and space. The Qur'an emphasizes the sanctity of time by specifying the number of months as twelve and totally forbidding the intercalation of the calendar. It identifies certain lands as sacred and others sacrosanct. Within this time-space frame one may come to understand the existence of man since the time of the creation of Adam and Eve until he reaches his ultimate destiny. This existence is the link between the universality of the Qur'an and that of humankind.

6. Recognition of an intrinsic Qur'anic rationale whose rules are infused in its text and that man is capable, with God's help, of uncovering the rules of this rationale that will guide his mind and his activity. These rules themselves are capable of becoming laws that protect the objective mind against deviation and perversity. The Qur'anic rationale can provide a common base for human intellectual activity. It would help man break away from the hegemony of his own thinking which is shaped by tradition and blind imitation of previous generations and the attendant tribal consequences.

7. Adopting the Qur'anic concept of geography. The whole earth belongs to God and Islam is the religion of God. In reality, every country is either a land of Islam (*dār al-Islām*) as a matter of fact, or will be so in the future. All humanity is the community of Islam (*ummat al-Islām*), either by adopting the faith or as a prospective follower of it.

8. Recognizing the universality of the Qur'anic mission. Unlike previous scriptures which addressed specific, localized communities, the Qur'an began by addressing Muhammad and his close family, then turned to Makkah and the surrounding towns, then to other communities, and finally to the whole of humankind. Thus, it became the only book capable of dealing with global situations. Any message to today's world must be based on common rules and values in a methodical way. It has to be based

on rules that govern objective thinking. Apart from the Qur'an, there is not a single scripture anywhere in the world today that can satisfy these requirements.

9. Studying very closely the complicated aspects of the lives of people, as the context within which questions and issues arise. Unless life is understood properly in all its dimensions, it will be difficult to formulate a suitable fiqh theory capable of referring to the Qur'an and obtaining satisfactory and correct answers. During the time of the Prophet, questions would arise out of various situations and revelation would be received providing the answers. Today, the Revelation is complete and all we need to do is articulate our problems and requirements and then refer to the Qur'an for answers. We then refer to the Sunnah of the Prophet to understand the context of the Revelation and link the text with the actual situation or incident.

10. Studying in detail the fundamental principles, especially those relating to the ultimate purposes of the Shariʿah, in order to incorporate them in the formulation of the principles of a modern fiqh for minorities. The study must be based on the ultimate purposes and linked to the governing higher values, noting the delicate distinction between the purposes of the Shariʿah and the intentions of responsible adults.

11. Recognizing that the inherited fiqh is not an adequate reference for fatwa or the formulation of rules in such matters. It does, however, contain precedents of fatwa and legislation which can be applied and referred to for determining approaches and methodologies, as appropriate. Whatever is found to be applicable, useful and representative of the spirit of Islam may be taken, preserving continuity with the past. This should be done without elevating the ruling to the level of Qur'anic text or taking it as an absolute for the issue in question. It is not a criticism of our predecessors that they did not have answers to issues they had not encountered or events and situations unheard of in their time.

12. Testing our fatwas, rulings and opinions in real-life situations. Every ruling of fiqh has its own impact on reality, which can be positive, if the fatwa is correctly deduced, or otherwise resulting in certain setbacks somewhere along the way. The outcome in the latter case would be negative and the ruling must be reviewed and revised. Thus, the fatwa process becomes one of debate and discussion between the fiqh and the realities of life which are the ultimate testing ground that will prove how appropriate and practical the fiqh really is.

KEY QUESTIONS

Jurists concerned with fiqh for minorities need to reflect very carefully on the key questions that arise from this subject, in order to prepare the ground fully and arrive at the true divine rulings, as far as humanly possible. These questions include the following:

1. How do members of minorities answer the questions: "Who are we?" and "What do we want?" in such a way that accurately reflects their particular situation and the common factors they share with others?

2. Under what political system is a particular minority living? Is it democratic, hereditary or military?

3. What kind of majority is the minority living with? Is it authoritarian, consumed by feelings of dominance and possessiveness? Is it a majority willing to achieve a dynamic balance based on carefully considered rules that guarantee minority rights? How significant are these guarantees, and what mechanisms are in place to secure them?

4. What is the size, or weight, of the minorities we are dealing with in respect of their human, cultural, economic and political abilities and resources?

5. What is the extent of the interaction between members of the society? Is there interaction between the minority and the majority in resources, industries, professions and activities (rights and obligations), or is there discrimination based on laws confirming and promoting separation and segregation in all these fields?

6. What is the nature of the human geography of the society? Are there any natural or artificial differences, disparities or distinctions? Are there certain natural resources peculiar to the minority or the majority, or are these resources common?

7. Has the minority any cultural dimension or identity that enables it, perhaps in the long run, to dominate culturally? What would be the effect of this upon the majority?

8. Has the minority an extended existence outside the shared land, or has it no external roots or extensions? What would be the effect in either case?

9. Has the minority any distinctive functions or activities it wishes to preserve, and what are they?

10. Is the minority able to perform these activities normally, or does that require institutions and leadership to organize?

11. What role do such institutions and leaders play in the lives of the minority? Do they highlight the minority's cultural identity?

12. Can such institutions turn into a network of interests that enhance the minority's distinctive qualities and persuade it that its cultural characteristics are the factors that identify it as a minority?

13. Would such institutions, unconsciously, lead members of the minority to question crucially the value or significance of these

distinctive features, and ask why they should not be passed on to others, or persuade the majority to adopt them?

14. If the minority is a blend of both the historic and the ethnic, how can its identity be defined without risking its people being absorbed into the majority or becoming self-centered?

15. How can the minority be educated to deal with the reactions of the majority and absorb the negative fallout without forfeiting the benefits?

16. How can common activities between the minority and the majority be developed and promoted? What areas have to be taken into account in this regard?

17. How can the "special" and the "common" cultural identities be preserved and brought together at the same time?

18. What must the minority do in order to identify those parts of its culture that could become common? What parts of the majority culture can it adopt? What is the majority's role in this process?

According to these clarifications, which relate to the approach and the objectives as well as to the key questions that arise, we can argue that many of the old opinions which emerged during the times of the empires will not, with all due respect, be of much use to us in establishing a contemporary fiqh for minorities. We nevertheless acknowledge the benefit many of them had specific to their time and place. We must go back to Revelation and the first Islamic model, taking note of the contributions of some fiqh practitioners whose opinion reflected the true spirit of Islam and who succeeded more than others in transcending the restrictions of history. Such opinions, however, cannot be taken as a source for Islamic rulings.

A FUNDAMENTAL RULE IN MUSLIM RELATIONS WITH OTHERS

The following two Qur'anic verses express the golden rule defining the relationship between Muslims and others:

> God does not forbid you to be kind and equitable to those who have neither fought you on account of your religion nor driven you from your homes. God loves the equitable. But God only forbids you to be allies with those who have fought you because of your religion and driven you from your homes and abetted others to do so. Those that make friends with them are wrongdoers. (*al-Mumtaḥanah*: 8–9)

Ibn al-Jawzī says: "This verse permits association with those who have not declared war against the Muslims and allows kindness towards them, even though they may not be allies."[27] Al-Qurṭubī says: "This verse is a permission from God to establish relations with those who do not show hostility towards the believers or wage war against them. It states that God does not forbid you to be kind to those who do not fight you."[28] Ibn Jarīr al-Ṭabarī pointed out the general reference to non-Muslims of other religions and creeds. He says: "The most credible view is that the verse refers to people of all kinds of creeds and religions who should be shown kindness and treated equitably. God referred to all those who do not fight the Muslims or drive them from their homes, without exception or qualification."[29]

The majority of commentators understood "equity" to mean also justice. However, Qāḍī Abū Bakr ibn al-ʿArabī was of a different view because justice is incumbent on Muslims in the treatment of everyone, friend or foe. He cites the Qur'anic statement: "Let not a people's enmity towards you incite you to act contrary to justice; be just, for it is closest to righteousness" (*al-Mā'idah*: 8). Ibn al-ʿArabī understands "equitable" in this context to mean benevolent, by showing financial generosity towards non-Muslims, whereas justice is expected towards those who fight the Muslims as well as those who do not.[30]

These two verses set out the moral and legal foundation principle with which the Muslims must comply in their dealings with people of other faiths: kindness and justice towards all non-belligerent communities. All developments and new situations must be judged according to this principle. The relationship between Muslims and non-Muslims cannot deviate from the main framework. The essential purpose for which God has revealed His words and sent His messengers is the establishment of justice in the world. The Qur'an says: "We have sent Our messengers with manifest signs and sent down with them the Book and the balance, that people may act with justice" (*al-Ḥadīd*: 25). This is an incontrovertible universal principle which applies with respect to the rights of Muslims and non-Muslims alike.

A RAISED NATION

The Qur'an also describes the Muslim community as the "best nation ever raised for humankind" (*Āl ᶜImrān*: 110). This statement indicates that the qualities of the Muslim nation reside in the fact that God has raised it to lead humankind out of darkness and into the light, from servitude to man to submission to God Almighty, as expressed by Rabīᶜ ibn Amīr (a Muslim representative) when he addressed the Shah of Persia (Rustum). It is a nation that has been raised in order to lead others and whose nature and role on earth are intertwined.

Commentators, past and present, have pointed out this link between the nature and the role of the Muslim community. In explaining this statement, ᶜIkrimah says: "The best of mankind [is] for mankind. In the past, people were not secure in other people's lands, but as Muslims, people of any color feel secure among you, as you are the best people for mankind."[31] Ibn al-Jawzī says: "You are the best people for mankind."[32] Ibn Kathīr says: "It means that Muslims are the best of nations and the most obliging towards other people."[33] Al-Naḥḥās and al-Baghawī also supports this view.[34] Abū al-Suᶜūd elaborates further saying: "You are the best community for people which clearly means helpful to other people. This is also implicit in the fact that the Muslim nation was raised for the benefit of mankind."[35] This is the same understanding expressed by al-Khaṭīb who says: "A feature of the Muslim nation is that it should not keep any beneficial advantage to itself but should share its benefit with other human societies."[36]

With these two qualities, the Muslim Ummah's role is not limited by land or confined in space. It has to reach out to others to convey the message of God. Thus, all references to *dār al-kufr* or *dār al-Islām* or *dār al-ḥarb*, as geographical entities, become superfluous and restrictive.

Indeed, the concept of nation, or Ummah, in Islamic jurisprudence is not associated with a particular human group or geographical location. It is solely dependent on the principle, even if it revolves around a single person. Thus, the Qur'an refers to Ibrahim as being "a nation" in his own right. It says: "Ibrāhīm was a 'nation,' a paragon of piety, an upright man obedient to God. He was no polytheist, [for he was] always grateful for the blessings God gave him. God chose him and guided him to a straight path" (*al-Naḥl*: 120–121).

Some classical scholars had identified what we mean here and linked those limitations only to the possibility of Islam spreading wide and to the security of Muslims. Islam knows no geographic boundaries; *dār al-Islām* is anywhere a Muslim can live in peace and security, even if he lives among a non-Muslim majority. Likewise, *dār al-kufr* is wherever Muslims live under threat, even if the majority there adhere to Islam and Islamic culture.

Al-Kāsānī says: "Our [Ḥanafī] scholars are agreed that *dār al-kufr* could become *dār al-Islām* once Islamic law is applied there."[37] Qāḍī Abū Yūsuf and Muḥammad ibn al-Ḥasan said that *dār al-Islām* "becomes *dār al-kufr* if non-Islamic law is implemented."[38] Ibn Ḥajar cites a view of al-Māwardī in which he goes well beyond this and considers that it is preferable for a Muslim to reside in a country where he can practice his religion openly than living in *dār al-Islām* because he would be able to attract more people to his faith and introduce it to them, even if by merely living amongst them. Al-Māwardī says: "If a Muslim is able to practice his religion openly in a non-Muslim land, that land becomes *dār al-Islām* by virtue of his settling there. Settling in such a country is preferable to moving away from it as other people would be likely to convert to Islam."[39]

Imam Fakhr al-Dīn al-Rāzī was notably correct in citing al-Shāshī's views and taking them as a basis for introducing an excellent alternative to the classification of lands. Instead of *dār al-ḥarb*, he describes the whole world as *dār al-daʿwah*, or the land for the propagation of Islam, and *dār al-Islām* as *dār al-ijābah*, or the land of compliance. He also classifies people into *ummat al-daʿwah*, the non-Muslims, and *ummat al-ijābah*, the Muslims.

STANDING UP FOR ONE'S RIGHTS

God praised the believers for being positive and for standing up for their rights. He praised them for rejecting tyranny and injustice and for refusing to accept disgrace and humiliation. God says: "and those who avenge themselves when tyranny is incurred upon them help and defend themselves" (*al-Shūrā*: 39). Commenting on this verse, Ibn al-Jawzī says: "A Muslim must not allow himself to be humiliated."[40] Ibn Taymiyyah says: "The opposite of avenging oneself is despondency and the opposite of patience is despair; neither patience nor despair are laudable as we can see with many people, including religious ones who incur wrong-doing or witness abhorrent acts. They neither stand up and avenge themselves nor remain patient; they are in fact despondent and despairing."[41]

Hence, acquiescence by Muslims to humiliation, resignation to inferior positions, the adoption of negative attitudes towards others, or withdrawal from pro-active interaction with the environment they live in, would be in contradiction to the principles advanced by these Qur'anic statements that call for affirmative and constructive engagement.

FORBEARANCE

Even if the Muslim minority's pro-active participation with the majority should entail certain courtesies that may blur or dilute some aspects of the minority's behavior or qualities, other than the fundamentals of its faith, it would be acceptable and pardonable, because without such participation a greater good would be forfeited. This is not a new situation for Islamic fiqh. It was something that Muslim scholars have tolerated ever since the end of the era of the first four caliphs. Muslims were facing two choices: affirmative participation with certain concessions demanded by the reality of the prevailing tyranny, or passive association and withdrawal, leaving the Ummah easy prey for tyrants. They opted for the former because of what they knew of Islam's positive and flexible attitude.

In establishing this principle, Ibn Taymiyyah says: "Muslims are required to do their best to cope with the situation. Those who assume office with the intention of pleasing God and serving the objectives of Islam and the interests of the people to the best of their ability, and who try their best to prevent wrong-doing, will not be penalized for what they could not achieve. It is far better that good people are in office than bad ones."[42] He also said: "Wrong-doing and sinful behavior by some Muslims, rulers as well as subjects, should not prevent others from taking part in good activities."[43] Were he alive today, he would have said "some non-Muslims, rulers or subjects" in accordance with the rationale of legal balance he had adopted while taking into account the changing times.

By the same logic, Ibn Ḥajar accepted seeking office and canvassing for it, although it is prohibited by the Sunnah if Muslim interests are threatened or liable to be harmed or squandered. He said: "Taking office for fear of waste is akin to giving without being asked as this is usually done with no personal greed. Such desire can be overlooked for those who should take office as it becomes an obligation upon them."[44]

LESSONS FROM THE EMIGRATION TO ABYSSINIA

During the early days of Islam, a number of Muslims took refuge in the non-Muslim land of Abyssinia in order to preserve their faith. This episode bears particular significance because it occurred at a time when Muslims were as weak as they are today, and while the foundations of Islamic law and fiqh were still being established.

An interesting incident took place during this episode which provides evidence for what Muslim immigrants can do to protect their faith and their interests, gain the confidence and trust of others and draw their attention to Islam.

In his *Musnad*,[45] Imam Aḥmad includes several reports of a lengthy account of how the Quraysh Arabs decided to harass the Muslim immigrants in Abyssinia. They dispatched ʿAmr ibn al-ʿĀṣ and ʿAbd Allah ibn Abī Rabīʿah brimming with gifts and presents to the Negus of Abyssinia and with sweeteners for his patriarchs in an effort to persuade him to hand over the Muslim refugees so that they could forcibly return them to Makkah.

First ʿAmr spoke at the Negus's court and then ʿAbd Allah, saying:

> "Your Majesty, a few of our foolish youths have come to your country and deserted the religion of their people but have not embraced your faith. They have come up with a new religion which neither you nor we understand. The nobles of their people, their fathers, uncles and tribesmen have sent us to you asking for them back because they know better what is best for them and what they had done wrong, and had already admonished them."

His patriarchs endorsed what was said and advised the king to hand the Muslims over to them to take back to their country and their people. However, being a fair man, the Negus would not take a decision without hearing the argument of the other side, and so asked for the Muslims to be brought before him.

When his emissary went to them, the Muslims sought the counsel of one another as to what to say to the Negus when he met them. They decided to tell him all that they knew and what their Prophet had taught them, no matter what the consequences. They went to him and he called his bishops and prelates who sat with their holy books open before them. He started by asking the Muslims: "What is this religion that caused you to break away from your people without converting to my religion or to any of the other religions?"

Umm Salamah reported that Jaᶜfar ibn Abī Ṭālib answered him and said:

> "O King, we were a people living in ignorance, worshipping idols, eating carrion meat, committing sins, forsaking our kinsfolk and abusing our neighbors. The strong amongst us exploited the weak. We had been living like that until God sent us a Messenger, one of us, whose pedigree, truthfulness, honesty and purity are well-known to us. He called us to believe in the one God and worship Him and discard the stones and idols we and our fathers had hitherto been worshipping besides Him. He urged us to be truthful in what we say, keep our trust, nurture our kinsfolk, be kind towards our neighbors and desist from offensive behavior and killing. He advised us to avoid repugnant acts, falsehood, taking orphans' property and slandering chaste women. He urged us to worship God alone and nothing else besides Him, and taught us to observe prayer, give alms and fast. We believed him and followed his teachings, but our people set upon us and persecuted us to turn us away from our religion and take us back to idol-worship and the repugnant acts we used to commit. When they overwhelmed and oppressed us and prevailed over us, preventing us from practicing our religion, we came to your country and chose you over all others, desirous to live as your neighbors and hoping, O King, not to be persecuted in your land." Other reports point out that, on appearing before the King, Jaᶜfar departed from convention and did not prostrate himself before the Negus. When asked by the Negus's courtiers why he did not prostrate, he replied: "We prostrate before no one but God Almighty."

The debate ended with the Muslims scoring victory over their opponents and the Negus was persuaded of the justice of their case. The Quraysh emissaries returned home "humiliated and their argument totally rejected," as Umm Salamah had put it. Following this episode, relations between the Muslims and Abyssinia's Christian monarch flourished to the extent that they would pray for his victory against other contenders for his throne. Umm Salamah said: "We prayed to God to help the Negus prevail over his rivals and confirm his rule in his country." The logical consequence of that relationship was that the Negus eventually embraced the religion of Islam.

CONCLUSION

IT should be clear from this brief monograph that the Islamic fiqh relating to Muslim minorities is essentially derived from the general fiqh of Islam as a whole. It is in a similar category to the fiqh of fundamentals, priorities (*al-awlawiyyāt*), contrasts (*al-muwāzanah*), or realities, or to comparative fiqh, or the fiqh of ethics etc. Accordingly, although this branch of fiqh includes several aspects of the general fiqh, it focuses specifically on issues affecting Muslim minorities living among non-Muslim majorities and endeavoring to preserve their identities under somewhat different customs, legislation and laws. It is also common knowledge that every fiqh ruling has its own cultural impact. Indeed, culture stems from fiqh and the laws that govern society. Fiqh and religious rulings also raise questions in an uninterrupted circle of arguments and interpretations, where fiqh, religious legislation and culture all play interchangeable roles. A number of methods, means and tools do exist with which this fiqh can be constructed on sound foundations, and these include the following: "Fiqh for Minorities" is a collective discipline and should not be practised on an individual basis. It is multifaceted, with differing aspects that render any individualistic approach potentially perilous. It comprises political, economic, cultural, social and legal elements. The fiqh side of it requires appropriate treatment of facts and issues. No treatment can be correct without consideration of all aspects of the matter in question, a task that cannot be completely fulfilled by a single individual. It requires the collective input of several scientists and specialists from different social and religious disciplines. These people need to scrutinize and study the issue from all angles, especially those of a general nature, that affect the future of Muslim minorities, in order to articulate the problems accurately and seek their solutions in fiqh. Indeed, the fiqh derived for these cases should not be based on partial evidence or facts commonly approved by jurists, but should be broadly based on the universal fundamentals of the Qur'an and Sunnah, as well as the established values and objectives (*maqāṣid*) of the Shariʿah. It is, therefore, a varied discipline that can be encompassed or fully understood, as already pointed out, only by someone with a vast knowledge and experience of all other aspects and branches of fiqh.

Specialist seminars can be an effective forum for the development of a minorities fiqh, provided that they are well planned, enough time is allocated to them, and are well attended by specialists, researchers and scholars. The aim is to articulate the various aspects of this field and provide satisfactory answers that can help define the identity of minorities.

Some issues may be developed into research projects for further and deeper study and investigation, with the necessary time and effort devoted to the task. Some issues may be recommended for academic degree studies at university level, supervised by experts or professors with a specialist knowledge in the field. For example, a question regarding economics could be dealt with jointly by an economist, a legal expert and a religious jurist, each dealing with the subject from his/her specialist angle. It is essential to bear in mind here that language and linguistics have an important and profound bearing on the formulation of the subject under study and its articulation from the fiqh point of view.

When seeking or giving fatwas, especially with respect to Muslim minorities, it is generally advisable to accustom people to submitting their questions in writing. A written question is more likely to receive greater attention and be given deeper thought. Specialists responding to these questions are also advised to give written answers to avoid any misunderstanding or misapprehension. People usually interpret things according to their wishes rather than with due objectivity. When inquirers pose their questions in their own particular way, the respondent jurists ought, nevertheless, to ask them to repeat them in writing, even if both parties are on the same wavelength.

Writing usually entails focusing and reflection, and allows the inquirers to mull over the issues and have greater confidence in explaining their ideas. If the respondents then wish to discuss or clarify those ideas with the inquirers, either over the telephone or face to face, to help the inquirers understand fully the implications of their questions, that is all the better. The respondents, on the other hand, are also required to write down their responses to avoid any misuse or misinterpretation of either the letter or the spirit of their answers. This should provide the necessary safeguards for the accuracy and integrity of the questions as well as the answers.

It is also imperative that people are made aware of the importance of fatwas and their impact on the future of Muslim minorities and their relationships with other communities in society, as well as the image of Islam in their own minds and the prospect of its application to them. A fatwa may solve a specific or short-term difficulty for some individuals, but raise several others that go beyond individual cases to affect the current and future state of the community as a whole. This awareness of possible conclusions and consequences further emphasizes the need to take account of the principles of the fiqh of priorities and consequences, as well as its other branches, in a manner that is conducive to the correct application of the tenets of Islam.

Jurists must also be fully aware of their environment and their cultural and social surroundings. Some questions on the nature of the minority and the majority living in this environment have already been identified. Fiqh practitioners need to understand these very well to be able to offer appropriate answers that take account of all the surrounding conditions. They must also submit their findings to those directly concerned as well as to other members of the community in the mosques and elsewhere, so that their meaning and implications are fully and clearly understood.

There is also the question of who is most qualified to contribute to the development of fiqh for minorities. We believe that it would be more effective to develop existing institutions and associations of Muslim social scientists, within which departments of fiqh and Shariʿah for students and practitioners could be established. This would enable traditional jurists and modern social scientists to co-operate and work closely together towards the achievement of the objectives that we have been advocating. This would initiate a debate between the two groups, in which knowledge of the Shariʿah sources can be passed on to social scientists. Similarly, various dimensions of modern social studies that have eluded Muslim jurists may be identified and clarified.

We do not believe that fiqh councils, as they exist today, are adequate, especially since they reproduce old fatwas in contemporary language or use current vernacular. We require original interpretations which respond to the problems of minorities in a way that is free of the negative effects that are usually associated with the fiqh of expediency or crises. For Muslim minorities to be offered solutions to their problems only on the basis of expediency or exceptionality can have harmful consequences that they should be spared of. The solution is for groups of experts with differing specializations to come together under the auspices of the associations of social sciences and Islamic studies. They should collaborate on an equal basis without any group being given the impression that it is being exploited or marginalized by the others. In any case, as questions of a political, economic, educational, philosophical or ethical nature arise, specialists from all sides can be called upon to examine jointly the religious and social aspects of the issues. This arrangement, in our view, would be more effective than fiqh councils limited only to Shariʿah experts.

Factors of time and space also play an important role in the determination of the nature of the issues being discussed. This is reflected in keeping the field of Muslim minorities fiqh open for development so as to take account of new circumstances in an ever-changing human condition. This applies to all areas of fiqh, whether macro or micro. The Islamic system is fundamentally open, and changing circumstances do affect the nature of the issues and questions being encountered and put forward. It is often true that these vary even within the same country and the same era. The Muslim minorities fiqh should not, therefore, remain rigid or restricted, but ought to be open to ijtihad and debate whenever factors emerge that had not previously existed, or were overlooked, when the question was initially raised.

The Islamic system is an open system in which no final word can be said unless it is a fact already established. As long as the subject matter is within the boundaries of ijtihad, it should be open to speculation, debate and amendment as and when new facts or factors emerge.

The methods and procedures necessary for a fiqh for Muslim minorities should be developed in a number of areas. Some of these relate to the individual or a body or a council issuing or applying the fatwa; some to the group or community for which the fatwa is issued. For this project to take proper shape and to make the public more aware of the establishment of a fiqh system, we need to respond better to people's problems. We also need to build up a repertoire of knowledge that will enable us to deduce objective principles defining the sources of knowledge and thought models, and the essential features of Islamic fiqh for Muslim minorities. To this end, further and wider studies, research and elaboration are required. This holds true for specific cases as well as the cultural, social and legal existence of Muslim minorities in their communities. It is over and above the definition of the fiqh components common to general fiqh and the fiqh of the minorities and the areas of distinction and specialization between them.

This type of investigation and research would make this fiqh useful not only for the Muslim minorities but also for the Muslim majorities, who could apply it to their own advantage.

Finally, what we have said so far regarding the fiqh of Muslim minorities is a mere introduction, intended to provoke interest in issues peculiar to Muslim minorities. Since this fiqh is open to debate and discussion, so should be its development, the documentation of its literature and the elaboration of its means, methods and tools. These must be open to researchers, scientists, religious scholars and intellectuals. The author will be happy to receive from readers any suggestions or comments that may assist in further research and analysis.

NOTES

1 Died, 227AH.
2 See Yaqūt al-Ḥamawī, *Mu^cjam al-Buldān*, 6/226.
3 Refer to the Prophet's Hadith: "...the whole earth has been made a residence and a place of worship for Me [Allah]..."
4 Cf Shakib Arsalan, *Tarīkh Ghazawāt al-^cArab* (Beirut: Dār Maktabat al-Ḥayāt, 1966).
5 Cf Fakhr al-Dīn al-Rāzī, *al-Tafsīr al-Kabīr*, in which he uses a different concept for "earth" which I have further developed in order to disregard the concepts of *dār al-ḥarb* and *dār al-Islām*. This distinction will be detailed later. Dr. Radwan al-Sayyid, the Lebanese scholar, has used similar concepts like *dār al-da^cwah* and *dār al-ijābah* or *ummat al-da^cwah* and *ummat al-ijābah* in many of his writings.
6 Among the books dealing with this is, *al-Mi^cyār al-Mu^carrab wa al-Jāmi^c al-Mugharrab ^can Fatāwā Ifrīqyah wa al-Andalus wa al-Maghrib*, by Aḥmad ibn Yaḥyā al-Wansharīshī (died 914AH) (Beirut: Dār al-Gharb al-Islamī, 1983).
7 ṢAAS—*Ṣalla Allāhu ^cAlayhi wa Sallam*: May the peace and blessings of Allah be upon him; said whenever the name of Prophet Muhammad is mentioned or whenever he is referred to as the Prophet of Allah.
8 For a new enlightened approach to this issue see AbdulHamid AbuSulayman, *Marital Discord: Recapturing Human Dignity Through the Higher Ojectives of Islamic Law* (London: IIIT, 2008). [Editors].
9 Ibn Khaldūn, *al-Muqaddimah*, p. 445; see also al-Zubaydī, *Tāj al-^cArūs*; al-Qarāfī, *Nafā'is al-'Uṣūl, Sharḥ al-Maḥṣūl, Ṭabaqāt Ibn Sa^cd fī Tarjamat Ibn ^cUmar*; Mustafa Abd al-Raziq, *Al-Imām al-Shāfi^cī*, and *Silsilat A^clām al-Islām*.
10 Ibid. p. 446.
11 *Ṣaḥīḥ al-Bukhārī: Kitāb al-^cIlm*, hadith no. 69; *Ṣaḥīḥ Muslim: Kitāb al-Zakah*, hadith no. 1719.
12 *Ṣaḥīḥ Muslim*.
13 al-Nassā'ī, Ibn Mājah, and al-Tirmidhī. See also *Al-Muwaṭṭa' of Imam Mālik* by Imam Mālik ibn Anas. Translated by Aisha

Bewley. 23:4 "Storing Meat from Sacrificial Animals."

14 • Grandfather's inheritance. One group considered the grandfather as a 'father' and placed him above the brothers. They also differed whether he is entitled to 'one third' or 'one sixth' of the estate.
• Suspension of the share of new converts. The Prophet and Abū Bakr included them in Zakah, but ʿUmar did not, possibly in the public good.
• Adjusting the distribution of booty. The Prophet divided the land gained in war among the fighters, while ʿUmar decided to charge a levy for its cultivation to benefit the whole community and the coming generations.
• Suspension of Shariʿah penalties (*ḥudūd*) in war times. Some Muslim leaders did it to avert defection to the enemy camps.
• Forgoing hand amputation for destitute thieves. ʿUmar pardoned thieves who stole to eat.
• Opting for compensation (*diyyah*) for murder following pardon by some relatives, even if others insisted on the death penalty (*qiṣāṣ*). The *Ṣaḥābah* encouraged pardon and compensation rather than the death penalty.
• During the Prophet's life, *diyyah* was valued in cash rather than cattle. ʿUmar, however, valued *diyyah* in camels because their market value had risen.
• During ʿUmar's time, stray camels were allowed to roam. When ʿUthmān succeeded him, he ordered that they be valued and traded. If the owner turned up, he was paid the market price for his camels. This was due to new circumstances resulting from the expansion of the Islamic state.
• While acknowledging it was not forbidden (*ḥarām*), ʿUmar disallowed marrying Jewish and Christian women.
• A single pronouncement of divorce was considered final up to the first two years of ʿUmar's reign. But then he concluded that people were abusing the rule and instituted three pronouncements for an irrevocable divorce.
• Imposing fines on manufacturers if they damage or destroy the raw material supplied to them, was an issue for debate. Some *Ṣaḥābah* were of the opinion that a penalty equivalent to the value of the damages or lost material should be imposed; others took the opposite view provided the damage or loss are not intentional.
• Benefiting from a security. This was a matter for different views among the *Ṣaḥābah*, dictated by different environments and social developments.

15 Issues over which the second generation had different opinions:
• They opted for penalizing the security holder in case of loss or damage, equivalent to the value of the security.

• The Prophet recommended women to frequent mosques for prayer, but the second generation ᶜ*ulamā'* preferred them not to do so at night.

• Pricing of goods was rejected by the Prophet, but the second generation ᶜ*ulamā'* allowed it to protect the ordinary public.

• A divorcee who defaults on his divorce commitments is considered unfit to give witness in legal matters.

• Second generation ᶜ*ulamā'* rejected witness statements of some relatives for fear of injustice or lack of impartiality.

16 AS—ᶜ*Alayhi al Salām* or ᶜ*Alayhim al Salām* (Upon him/them be the blessings of Allah). Said whenever a prophet other than Muhammad is mentioned by name.

17 See his book: *Iqtiḍā' al-Ṣirāṭ al-Mustaqīm Mukhālafat Ahl al-Jaḥīm.* See also Muṣṭafā ibn Muhammad al-Wardānī, *Al-Nahī* ᶜ*an al-Isti*ᶜ*ānah wa'l-Istinṣār fī Umūr al-Muslimīn bi Ahl al-Dhimmah wa'l-Kuffār.* Also a book by an anonymous author believed to have come from North Africa entitled: *Al-Ṣawāb fī Qibḥ Istiktāb Ahl al-Kitāb.*

18 *Al-Mustaṣfā* 1/3

19 Taha Jabir al-Alwani, *Uṣūl al-Fiqh al-Islāmī* (Herndon, Virginia: International Institute of Islamic Thought (IIIT), 1990).

20 See his book *Maqāṣid al-Sharī*ᶜ*ah al-Islāmiyyah* (Tunis: Al-Dār al-Tūnisiyyah, 1972).

21 See his book *Maqāṣid al-Sharī*ᶜ*ah* (Casablanca: Maktabat al-Waḥdah, 1963).

22 See his book *Naẓariyat al-Maqāṣid* ᶜ*ind al-Imām al-Shāṭibī* (Herndon, Virginia: IIIT, 1995)

23 See his book *Maqāṣid al-Sharī*ᶜ*ah* (Herndon, Virginia: IIIT, 1991).

24 See his book *Tamhīd li Tārīkh al-Falsafah al-Islāmiyyah* (Cairo: Lijnat al-Ta'līf wa al-Tarjumah wa al-Nāshir, 1966)

25 For further elaboration, see al-ᶜAlwānī, *The Islamization of Knowledge: Yesterday and Today* (Herndon, Virginia: IIIT, 1995); and *Missing Dimensions in Contemporary Islamic Movements* (Herndon, Virginia: IIIT, 1996), pp. 14–19.

26 RAA—*Raḍiya Allāhu* ᶜ*Anha*/ᶜ*Anhu* (May Allah be pleased with her/him). Said whenever a companion of the Prophet is mentioned by name.

27 Ibn al-Jawzī, *Zād al-Masīr*, 8/39.

28 Al-Qurṭubī, *Al-Jāmi*ᶜ *li Aḥkām al-Qur'ān*, 18/43.

29 Ibid. 28/43.

30 Ibid. 18/43.

31 *Tafsīr Ibn Abī Ḥātim*, 1/472.

32 Ibn al-Jawzī, *Zād al-Masīr*, 1/355.

33 Al-Ṣābūnī, *Mukhtaṣar Tafsīr Ibn Kathīr*, 1/308.

34 Al-Qurṭubī, *Al-Jāmi*ᶜ *li Aḥkām al-Qur'ān*, 4/171.

35 Abū al-Suᶜūd, *Irshād al-*ᶜ*Aql al-Salīm ilā Mazāyā al-Qur'ān al-*ᶜ*Aẓīm*, 2/70.

36 ʿAbd al-Karīm al-Khaṭīb, *Al-Tafsīr al-Qur'ānī*, 4/548.

37 Al-Kāsānī, *Badā'iʿ al-Ṣanā'iʿ*, 7/131.

38 Ibid.

39 Ibn Ḥajar, *Fatḥ al-Bārī*, 7/230.

40 Ibn al-Jawzī, *Zād al-Masīr*, 7/122.

41 Ibn Taymiyyah, *Al-Tafsīr al-Kabīr*, 6/59.

42 Ibn Taymiyyah, *Al-Siyāsah al-Sharʿiyyah*, p. 167.

43 Ibn Taymiyyah, *Minhāj al-Sunnah*, 4/113.

44 Ibn Ḥajar, *Fatḥ al-Bārī*, 13/126.

45 Details of this account are reported in *Al-Musnad*, hadiths 1649, 14039, 17109, and 21460.

GLOSSARY OF TERMS

Aḥkām: Prescriptions directly taken from the Qur'an and the Sunnah.

Ahl al-Dhimmah: Protected people who adhere to their faith. The people with whom a compact or covenant has been made, and particularly People of the Book. An individual of this class namely, a free non-Muslim subject of a Muslim state.

ʿĀlim: (pl. ʿalims or *ʿulamā'*): Islamic scholar. Literally, "one who knows, a scholar, a scientist." Commonly used for someone who has a thorough knowledge of Islam and its sources—the Qur'an and the Sunnah. An important characteristic of an *ʿālim* is that he/she is deeply conscious of God and stands in awe of Him.

Dār al-Daʿwah: The land where Islam is propagated. *Dār al-Ijābah*: The land of compliance. *Dār al-Islām*: "Land of Islam." The land where Islam is followed. *Dār al-Kufr*: The country where Islam is not followed.

Fahm: Understanding.

Fatwa: (pl. fatwas or *fatāwa*). A juristic opinion given by an *ʿālim*, *mufti*, or *mujtahid*, *faqīh* on any matter pertinent to Islamic law.

Fiqh: Literally, "understanding." Knowledge of Islam through its laws; science of the law of Islam. The term "fiqh" is sometimes used synonymously with Shariʿah. However, while fiqh is, to a large extent, the product of human endeavor, the Shariʿah is closely related to divine Revelation and knowledge which is only obtained from the Qur'an and the Sunnah.

Faqīh: (pl. faqīhs or *fuqahā'*). Specialists in Islamic jurisprudence (fiqh). A *faqīh* can also be a synonym for *ʿālim* meaning Islamic scholar.

Ghayb, al: That which is beyond the reach of human perception.

Ḥadith: (pl. hadiths or *aḥādīth*): The verbalized form of a tradition of the Prophet Muhammad constitutive of his Sunnah. The word Hadith when H is capitalized also applies to the sciences dealing with the Prophet's Tradition in all its aspects.

Ḥalāl: That which is lawful (legal and allowed), as distinguished from *ḥarām*, or that which is unlawful.

ʿIddah: The term of probation incumbent upon women in consequence of a dissolution of marriage, either by divorce or the death of her husband. After a divorce the period is three months, and after the death of her husband, four months and ten days. Both periods being enjoined by the Qur'an.

Ijtihad: Considering that the accepted juridical sources of Islam are valid for all time and space, ijtihad may be described as a creative but disciplined intellectual effort to derive legal rulings from those sources while taking into consideration the variables imposed by changing circumstances of Muslim society.

Jihad: Literally, "striving". Any earnest striving in the way of God, involving either personal effort, material resources, or arms, in order to install righteousness and eliminate evil, wrongdoing and oppression. *Jihad al-Akbar*: Literally "the greater jihad". Striving against the temptation of the *nafs* i.e. the struggle to improve oneself and one's character.

Maqāṣid: The ultimate aims, objectives and intents of the Shariʿah.

Maṣāliḥ: Public welfare and interest.

Shariʿah: The collective name for all the laws of Islam. It includes all the religious, liturgical, ethical and jurisprudential systems.

Sunnah: Literally, "a clear path or beaten track". Refers to whatever the Prophet said, did, agreed to, or condemned. The Sunnah is the second source of the Shariʿah after the Qur'an.

Talfīq: Concoction or piecing together.

Taqlīd: Uncritical adoption or imitation and following of a particular scholar or school of thought.

Tawḥīd: The act of affirming that Allah is the One and only God, the Absolute, Transcendent Creator, the Lord and Master of the worlds. For a detailed study see Ismaʿil Raji al-Faruqi, *Al Tawḥīd: Its Implications for Thought and Life*, (Herndon, VA: IIIT, 1992).

Tazkiyah: Purification.

Ummah: (pl. *umam*): Literally, a "community, nation." Specifically, the universal Muslim community.

ʿUmrān: *ʿUmrān* is taken to mean the cultivation and development of the world as the arena harnessed for discharging man's mission and the crucible for his trials, accountability and development.

Uṣūl: (sing. *aṣl*): Principles, sources, origins. *Uṣūl al-fiqh*: Science of Islamic jurisprudence, philosophy of law; and the methodology of deriving laws from the sources of Islam and of establishing their juristic and constitutional validity.

Zakah: Usually rendered as the 'poor-due' or legal charity, zakah is the obligatory sharing of wealth with the poor and the community at the yearly rate of 2.5% of appropriated wealth above a certain minimum. An individual's wealth can be in the form of cash, commodities, livestock, agricultural goods and other items.